Unspoken, Barely Written
A Teenage Torment

Toni Hodges
De'Vray Rogers

Unspoken, Barely Written: A Teenage Torment
Copyright © 2010 by Brown Essence, Inc.

Printed and bound in the United States of America. All rights reserved. No part of this book may be reproduced or transmitted in any form or by any means, electronic or mechanical, including photocopying, recording, or by an information storage and retrieval system- except by a reviewer who may quote brief passages in a review to be printed in a magazine, newspaper, or on the web – without permission in writing from the publisher.

BROWN ESSENCE, INC.
P.O. BOX 82462
CONYERS, GA 30013

Please visit our website at brownessence.com and let us know what you think.

Dedication

I would like to dedicate this book to my mother *Terri S. Hodges,* for being the strongest woman I know through the toughest times. You inspire me. To my father, *Anthony "Tony" Hodges,* for his support in everything that I do. My niece *La'Terra Joy Marie,* for brightening each and every day in my life. And to my two sisters *Jalisa D. Clay & Jasmine S. Clay* for supporting me throughout the years.

- Toni T. Hodges

I dedicate this book to my loving nephew, *Javion Malikai.* I pray that the corruption that is in this book is something he never has to go through. I pray that he is on the other side where the grass is greener. I also dedicate this book to *Yarved* and my family. I hope they know I will love them forever.

- De'Vray C. Rogers

Table of Contents

Unspoken, Barely Written 12

Scream 13

Everlasting Rain 14

Love Entity 15

Remember This 16

Strength in Words, Pain in Meanings 18

Serve My Words 21

Destruction 22

Portraying Lying Images 23

Dreams 24

Distress 26

Dear Fragile Heart 27

Toni Said 28

Dear Boy 29

Addressing Democracy 30

You Need To Know 32

Choices 33

Bail 34

Strengthen Me 35

Vanity 36

Positive Mind 38
Earthly Recognition:
Facing My Fellow Homo sapiens 39
They're Just Feelings 41
I'll Never Understand It 42
Sorry Mother 44
Cope 46
Even Though 47
Judgment 48
Wake Up 49
Hard to Forget Memories 50
Waiting for a Saint 52
Routine Argument 53
Unwanted Seed 54
His Eyes, His Lies 56
Elastic 57
No Choice 60
I Am 61
Second Best 62
Time 63
Say NO! 64
His Response 66
Irony 67
My Therapy Session 68

Will Love Ever Last	70
My Sister's Keeper	71
Yesterday When You Cried	74
Epiphany to Grow	75
A Time in History	76
Reasons for My Actions	78
I Spoke	79
My Blessings	82
Remember Her?	83
If I Could Only Pretend	84
I Wonder Why	85
Perplexing	86
Armed	88
Feel?	89
Pay Me No Mind	90
Forget the Pain	91
Explaining Him	92
My Nemesis: Death	94
This is Who I Am	95
The Silent Killer: Depression	96
Revolution	97
The Human Experience	98
Realization	100
I Wish Words Were Undefinable	101

Observing the Pain	102
Heaven is Smiling Down	103
Staying Put	104
Absolution	106
If You Can Hear Me, Come Back	107
The Ocean of Eternity	108
If God Reads Minds	110
FPD (Friendship Police Department)	111
Friends Disappear	114
Love is What They Said	115
Stand	116
Worry in My Soul	117
Different Life	118
Captivated	120
My Conscious	121
To the Burdened Man	123
To the Burdened Woman	124
Right through You	125
Closed Emotions	128
I See Me	129
All I Know	130
She Makes Me Feel	131
Maybe I Am	132
Money Can't Buy Dreams	133

I Begged For Your Hand	136
I Shouldn't Care	138
Fading Sun	139
Words are True	140
Mistakes Made	141
Contradiction Amendment	142
I Remember	144
I Wish You Would	145
Who Are You	146
My Heart Beat	147
A Joke Pushed too Far	148
Holding Interest	152
Don't Care Assumptions	153
Attacking My Emotions	154
My Mommy	156
How…	157
Saying Errors	160
Yarved Speaks	161
I Am Isolated	162
Crush	163
Never Would I	164
Giving Up	166
You Want	167
How Do You Heal?	168

Mother 170
Scars 171
Not Alone 174
Once 175
Life as a Misfit 176
Strength in Words, Pain in Meaning Pt. II 178

Unspoken, Barely Written

As I write this, I ask myself
"Why do I bother wasting my time writing these words if it goes unheard?"
My mind answers: "Because there's nothing like verbal assault, kill 'em with your words. It cuts deeper"
Well there you have it.
Get ready to die by the unspoken TRUTH
the realness packed into this ink.
Bursting through the seams, my thoughts are fiends,
craving to be written
to be acknowledged
I'm re-inventing the meaning
of creativity
its more than a rhyme with a simile
it's my identity
Now truthfully am I only imagining
that your eyes are deceiving me?
Reading this I'm sure you'll think
"What's with all this ranting?"
My mind is overflowing.
Thoughts are reproducing
In closing: this is all I feel
    - Toni

Scream

Abandoned
Isolated
Not a soul gives a damn
About this adolescent coated in imperfections
The people that I thought had my back
All stabbed a knife into it
Yet no one seems to notice
Suicidal mindset
Liquid hate beneath my eyelids
Mom & dad don't understand they never seem to see it
The situations that I'm in, they call 'em all excuses
Friends...
I never had
At least I thought I did
But they turn their backs when they see
How really hard it is

    - Toni

Everlasting Rain

This rain is everlasting
Staring out my window
Wondering if this earth shower will come to an end
This hurt inside me is festering
I wish that dark cloud above my head
Would stop hovering...
This rain rinses no pain
The coldness in my bones is keeping me restrained
The sadness in my soul is deepening
My heart is slowly weakening...
Many days the sun will shine.
The heat from the sun rays will only keep me inside.
This cold room of mine will witness the rain shower from my eyes.

- Toni

Love Entity

Wanting you kills the very core of me
Knowing that no matter what I say won't change a thing
Life won't let us be
Into my hands I want to scream
In my heart it hurts to beat
In my lungs it hurts to breathe
This feeling won't let go of me
You're glued into my memory
The thought of you is lingering
If only I had you as mine, because honestly
Just meeting you moved me
Touching you healed me
Kissing you changed me
You're more than my friend at a distance
You're my love entity

    - Toni

Remember This

If we can withstand the storm
We can manage through the night
Even in the bitterest of times
When the waterworks soak the pillowcase
& the memories are all scattered
In our minds like a collage
With no words to utter
So we feel miserable & dejected
Because we all want one thing
Rather we know it or not
It's undeniable
But to turn our backs on love
Hurts us the most

- Toni

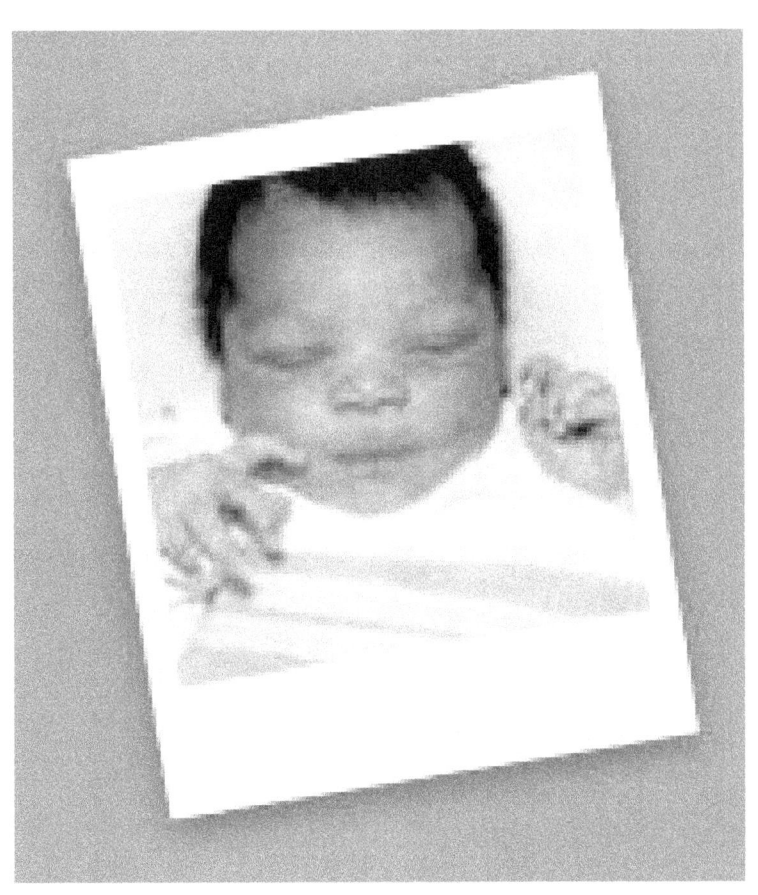

Strength in words
Pain in meanings

You realize that words have strength
But you don't realize the impact each word has on me
Whether counting the years
Or each wrong step that I take
And every time you don't get your way
You try to send me away
I feel the LOVE, mother
You look at me as if I'm the one
Who turned my back on you
You're the reason why my chest hurts when I breathe
You let him abuse me
I feel your apology for the first time
How am I supposed to trust you?
When you lied to me?
You told me that if you knew about it
You would make a change
But it's been THREE times and you just let it go
Telling me he didn't mean it
You let him choke me until I couldn't breathe
Who am I supposed to believe?
What's the real truth that you're trying to hide from me?
How do you want the best for me?
But you're the main one holding me back

When I'm trying to get my life on track
I'm not going through a change
I've been the same since I came out
I was mentally disturbed in elementary
In middle school I tried not to let it get to me
Now that I'm in high school
I'm corrupted into this feeling of love and hate
When I tell my life story people never wonder
Why I came to be this way
You're the only one who neglects my pain
Neglects the truth
You didn't protect me understandable
God gave you a second chance for me to trust you
You made the same mistake over and over again
How should I feel?
When there was never enough love to melt away
This icy pain that's covering my heart
Our relationship is sad and full of pain
But I'm not the only one to blame
Can you tell me?
How I don't have love for you up until now
I had no life outside of the family
I tried to ignore the pain
But when I thought of all the things I never got to say
It made me question God
Asking Him why He gave me emotions

That made me feel this way
I will never forget you
How could I?
The other 23 of me
Came from you

- De'Vray

Serve my words

My words have
Never served
Their intended purpose
It served pain
When it was intended
To heal
It served lost
When it was intended
To help us find
Ourselves
I pray
That one day
My words serve
Their intended purpose

- De'Vray

Destruction

I turned my back on God
And went with the path
Of my destruction
Now I am forced
To live with these thoughts
Of what could've been

- De'Vray

Portraying Lying Images

You sit yourself on a pedestal
Built from lies
Are you ashamed of who you really are?
Or what you're becoming?
Your back sat turned to us
But your mouth flipped the story
And made it seem
Like our backs sat turned to you

- De'Vray

Dreams

I tried to call on family
But damn where are they
I feel as if I'm a sinner
With a past
And no future
Could I be a saint
Oh God I might faint
If I have to wait to find out
My past haunts me
So I don't sleep
My nightmares
Seem so inviting
But when I come
They kill me
How do you think it feels
To close your eyes
And watch death unfold?

- De'Vray

Distress

Blood streaked wrists
Tear stained cheeks
The cuts that she makes
Are never too deep
Pain does not exist
Love is not enough
Everything is darkness
Will she overcome?

~ Toni

Dear Fragile Heart

I am truly sorry for what they put you through
Wearing you on my sleeve was a mistake
Those lying, conniving, manipulative abusers
Told you lies of how they love adore and
Will never leave you
Giving off false pretenses, speaking of foolish dreams
talking of everlasting friendship
You fell for it again, and over again, and again
What's it going to take for you to see?
There's no such thing as a fairytale fantasy
No happy stress free haven
They said you were safe in their arms, but they
trapped you & tortured you
You've been tossed around to all of them
Spat on, crushed, stabbed
dropped to the cold pavement
I promise to never put you through this again
I will secure you by putting this guard up locked & bolted
So, when the next comes around, he'll be on the outside
Sincerely, your keeper

- Toni

Toni said,

Since some of you are clueless to the language of truth
My thoughts will translate:
Toni said, She'll soak up your tears,
and challenge your fears
She said, To stand alone, trust no one,
make it on your own
Don't believe in lies,
detect the truth by scanning their eyes
Toni said, Loves just a word, faith is a must,
make your voice heard
She said, listen real close, this is critical, a-need-to-know
Don't conform, don't stand in the crowd
while the clowns perform
Toni said, use your words as a weapon,
your voice as a mike, the world's your mission
She said, step out of the dark, reveal your light,
that's trapped in your heart
Keep your minds open, let it air out, let the clones know,
this is our time now
Toni said, experience makes us wiser
and pain makes us stronger
She said, when the world turns their backs, walk the
other way, forget what's right turn left
~ Toni

Dear boy

I'm down here now
That's how low I've sunk
A few feet under you
You moved on but I'm still stuck
Underneath my world, it crashed onto me
Rubble & debris, I can barely see
Looking up at you
Tears seep through
My eyes are red
Your sky is blue
My heart is dark, empty, and cold
No light comes through
I'm haunted now
By the memory of you…

- Toni

Addressing Democracy

This so called Democracy; nothing but Hypocrisy.
Locking us away for the same
Crime you do behind scenes
Abiding by your rules & regulations
Has never been my forte'
You've been scheming and plotting
Against society like we're all fresh prey
Uncle Sam ain't no kin of mine
Nothing but a crook and a gambler
Reaching up under aged skirts and
Stalking streets like a peddler
Go shoot an innocent bystander in a
Third-world country for looking at you funny
Go make a deal with an assassin to take down
World leaders with your blood money
Go ahead and monitor over conversations,
Follow us across the nation
The day is approaching for our youth
To unchain our minds, un-tape our mouths
and speak TRUTH!
Our voices will be heard, you will not keep us quiet
and remember one day that, your Lies will spark
A worldwide RIOT!

You need to know

Do you know
How much paper I have used
To drown out this ink in my soul
Of worthlessness
This is book number three of poetry
And you would never believe
By how easy I make it seem
How hard this is for me
I never liked to share my emotions but I'm trying
Because you need to know them
Before that tombstone hits saying 1996-to-
Let me stop right there
I don't even want to think of it
When I look at me
I can't see anything
Because when I think of my self-worth
I see myself as if I'm nothing
And I'm ashamed because my ancestors fought for me
To feel that I'm something
I'm not afraid of death , I'm afraid of where I'm going
Because I've used up all Gods mercy
That he had left
    - De'Vray

Choices

I'll be there for you
Because I could never
Withdraw completely
Even though I never
Wanted to feel
Like I had to make a choice
Between family
I resign from my race
From my ethnicity
And every tie I have to it
Because it's crazy
That I have to choose
Between you and her

- De'Vray

Bail

I am a child
That's gotten lost in the clouds
With dreams so wild
Nobody could believe
Nobody could conceive
the things
I went through
And I'm still dreaming
Speaks for itself
When I should
Have given up
I stayed to see
What would happen
But wave the white flag
And throw in the towel
Because this pain I bear
Has me sinking into the ground
Hello satan
It's funny seeing you around
Yes, I'm at my lowest
But maybe I'll wait
Just to see if God comes and bails me out
   - De'Vray

Strengthen me

If all things are possible
Then Christ strengthen me
Cause these tears
These sleepless nights
Have left me weak
I have exhausted
All my options
So for the first time
In a couple of weeks
I'll get down on my knees
And pray that
Christ strengthens me

- De'Vray

Vanity

How could you
Accept our pain
Then turn around
And make your own words vain
Last night I cried
Because I couldn't
Stand to look you in the face
I cried
Because I felt
As if it was my fault
For holding you to blame
For my shame
But tonight
I'm crying because
I'm trying to
But I can't forgive you
Because you forgave yourself
Then left it alone
As if it wasn't an issue

    - De'Vray

Positive Mind

Feels as though when I think of you, I cry
Why am I mourning, when you're very much alive?
Blurred eyes gaze at your picture like an obituary
What happened to that bond
We shared over conversations?
And the heat of the embrace we had full of emotion?
Was it all for nothing?
Am I just a shadow beside my own self being?
You left me half-dead without a heart
Where'd you put it?
Though we're a few miles away
It seems we're a thousand miles apart
Yet the distance is filled with tears
Flooding from my eyes
I can't swim and I'm drowning
My only life saver is a phone call away
Would you make it?

~ Toni

Earthly Recognition:
Facing My Fellow Homo sapiens

Confusing
Nonetheless effortless
How I (She) reject the emotions
Containing all things I'm in dire need of
For example love, trust
I'm familiar with those terms being one in the same
Refusing to trust the people you thought were love
Mistaking their identity as nothing but scum
Tasting the essence of freedom peace
Tranquility has become a needed drug
The fire that once burned and stemmed my desires
Were washed away and perished by my selfish tears
A stream of anguish turned into hatred
While the sanity of humanity faaaaadess.....
As though it was an echo beating the walls of our minds
This media is a curse
Brought onto the weakest brain membrane,
Telling us to embrace the images on the screen and
The sounds from the speakers
Little do we know
Mankind will be extinct by the hands of themselves
Ourselves
Revoke the deal and forfeit the game

Because in the end of our days
Only our souls will remain

- Toni

They're just feelings:

My clumsy emotions falls out of their hiding place.
Disheveled scattered before you.
Stepping over them you say "they're just feelings"
Well, these feelings were once buried deep in a place no one had yet to discover,
until you came and drained them in array
My soul crept out of its cave and shone a light on you
A light you drowned with darkness
Uncontrollably I stumbled into your hands
But you let me fall along with these emotions
Now here I am gathering them in a pile
Attempting to find them a better home
While you repeat "They're just feelings"

- Toni

I'll never understand it:

I'll never know how she does it but, I do know one thing
I will never understand it
How she puts up with his disrespect and spitefulness
The way he speaks of her, you'd think his words were
bullets and his tongue was cocked and loaded
Aiming at this woman's dim soul
Attempting to break her to the lowest point
As though hurting the one he loves
heals the wounds he obtained
As if, speaking of her in such a vulgar manner would
magically reconstruct his damaged heart
I'll never understand his pain
Or understand why he feels the way he does and
Why this woman's actions impacts him so deeply
This man has had a load of trouble battling his demons
and carrying his burden on his own
Together, she, a troubled woman with a wild past filled
with relentless mayhem
Him, a dysfunctional bitter man, with a dark past filled
with depression and hidden secrets
buried so deep even he couldn't dig it up
Together, along with their major blowouts in the
dawn of day or the dusk of night
Creates bruises on the minds of three little girls

This became a world of chaos they never should have been a part of...

- Toni

Sorry Mother

I can hear the sound of her tears falling
Washing over everything
Flooding the streets and homes of many
I can hear the sound of her growl and heavy breath
Blowing everything in her path into a mess
I can feel her anger
      Her sadness
           An overwhelming world of madness
I sit and watch what she's done
On the screen it reads: **BREAKING NEWS!**
Another worldwide catastrophe
She's done it again
Destroying homes
Releasing a blast of wretchedness
Mixed with death and turmoil
Yet she has every right to feel wrathful
We are a negative society...
      Sorry Mother Nature

- Toni

Cope

His pain
I know it well
Cause it's those same tears
That fell from my face
He's hurt
I can see it clearly
Cause I was hurt
I'm still hurt
And I want you to know
No matter how hard you try
You can't reverse time
But I forgive you
Because you didn't know
And I love you
Because no matter what
You always tried to help me
Cope

- De'Vray

Even though

I'm not his
I'll show him a side of me
That I once feared
To show anybody
That under this tough exterior
There's a soft inside
Even though I'm damaged
I'm a good guy
If I had the choice
I know if I had the time
I would rebuild
Every bridge that's been burned
In my life time

- De'Vray

Judgment

They judge me
And spit on my name
They tried to hurt me
And now they wonder
Why that finger won't go down

- De'Vray

Wake up

I wish you could
Have seen me after
I woke up
I was dazed
I actually believed
That I couldn't do better
That drug dealers
Had to live vicariously
Through me
Because of all the pain
You brought me
God, I wish you
Could've seen me
When I woke up

- De'Vray

Hard to forget memories

It's hard to forget
What we had
The memories that made me smile
Now they just make me sad
I feel like I'm the one to blame
For how we fell apart
Cause only you and God knows
That I was messed up
From the start

- De'Vray

Waiting for a Saint

I sit here
In a remote room overshadowed by darkness
With my knees pulled up to my chin
My eyes; Bloodshot and cheeks wet in streaks
Gazing into the abyss
Waiting for a saint to burst through my door in urgency
To save me from myself
I'm detrimental to my health
The sight of the wounds unhealed brought to light
Puts a bitter taste in my mouth
Regret, guilt, and sorrow
So I hide in the darkness
Waiting for that saint, to walk down my hallway
Could it be today?
Because it's a long way till tomorrow

- Toni

Routine Argument

The clock shows 3:02a.m.
Lying in my bed with the sheets pulled up to my nose
I could hear the rumble in the next room
Shouts of anger directed at my mother as she cried
"You'll wake the kids"
Beneath her drenched eyes
Reveals a life of demise kept hidden in her mind
As my father stares upon her,
Suspiciousness covers his face
All he ever knew was to love with hate
The accusations against her, he seems to believe in
But, she swears it's all in his head
She keeps repeating
"Everything is fine, baby go back to bed"
He shouts louder, she shouts in return
Now my future relationships, are based on what I learned

- Toni

Unwanted seed

I was 15
In the backseat of his Civic
I decided I was grown
And ended up with morning sickness
Arriving at the clinic
Doctor says I'm expecting
In my mind I'm thinking
"This is the end of my life!"
As I look at my parents,
There's disappointment in their eyes
I go to school the following morning
And it seems as though everyone knows
I was nervous but,
I told Him over the phone
The very next second I'm hearing a dial tone
Crying into my hands,
I calculate a plan
Back to the clinic, feeling relief
I want out with this thing
Living inside of me
I spread my legs, squeezing my eyes closed
"We're done here" says the Doctor
The seed is now gone

Walking out in shame, with my head hung low
And each and every day, my guilt still shows

- Toni

His eyes, his lies

You said you never met her
But, your eyes say otherwise
I mastered how to detect when you lie
You said you never met her
But, your lies say otherwise
Experience taught me the words that you speak
Are not really what they seem

- Toni

Elastic

In my innermost being
I've concealed my emotions
To prove that I am resilient
Against my own weaknesses

- Toni

No choice

I felt like they left me
With no choice
But to smoke and drink
Until the verbal scars
They gave me were gone
Till my body went numb
I couldn't feel anything
Emotionally, mentally, physically
Anymore

-De'Vray

I am

I'm stronger
Than I was before
I'm smarter
Than you ever were
And when you look
Back in my life
You're gonna regret
You ever broke my heart

- De'Vray

Second best

My dreams
Are fulfilling themselves
But why can't
I stop working myself?
I can't get comfortable
Even though I've already made it
For some reason
I still look at myself
Like I'm second best

- De'Vray

Time

I think that its time
For me to go
But honestly I don't know
If that would help me
Make better
Or just help me
Feel better

- De'Vray

Say NO!

She can't say no
She would rather lie
But in the end
That hurts me more
Than the truth ever would
I wonder
What goes through her head
When she truly believes
That lying to me
Is something she's forced to do
Maybe I should, enforce the law
Of honesty
Because honestly
She seems to be a "want"
Not a "necessity"
In my life

- De'Vray

His response

I can't trust myself with loving you
Because I'm afraid of hurting you
As much as I want to be with you
Something is telling me it's the wrong thing to do
And I don't want to lead you on,
As much as I already have
And I don't want to get too close with you,
Close enough to get attached
Being friends with you is hard
Because I do want you bad
It's just you're too young
Can you understand that?

-Toni

Irony

It's been a while Mr. Razor
Almost two years
Our anniversary has passed
I missed you
My skin missed you too
All the memories we shared
When I would get angry
I can always count on you to help me cope
My mom hates you
She says you're trouble
I disagree
I tried to substitute other things in place of you
No one or anything can release my anguish like you can
No therapy group meetings or anything
You are my knight and shining razor
I need you right about now
So let's meet up
My wrist is going to cry when she sees you again!

- Toni

My therapy session

Sitting in a chair in the corner of the room, a psychologist mentally evaluates my sanity.
Therapy session part 1:
Therapist: Hi Toni, so tell me your thoughts at this very moment
Me: Well to be truthful, I rather be sitting in a room with the walls closing in on me then answer your pointless questions
Therapist: And why do you feel this way?
Me: Because, you all think you're high and mighty.
Sitting in your chair, with your pen and paper
Looking down on me
Writing down what you think you heard, judging me off what I really said. Then running back to tell people with sticks up their butt.
Just so they can diagnose me as being
Mentally disturbed
Why? Because, I rather stand alone, instead of walking with the "In Crowd" "The Normal" & "The Fakes"?
You all are made up of plastic fibers concocted of misbeliefs you inherited from your forefathers
"The Liars"

I may have been born into a world of clones but I came
out uniquely defined, so while all of you have blonde hair,
blue eyes, I have gold specks in mine
You all looked at me as though I was different,
though different I am not.
I'm proof, that this world is non- existent.
We LIVE within OURSELVES.

- Toni

Will love ever last?

Love never lasts
Like an incomplete beat your heart makes
Through your chest at a steady pace
Then like a whisper in the night it slowly fades
Gradually resuscitating the thumping increasing
You're breathing...
the sharp edge of his words lodged real deep
Internally bleeding
His hate still stings
So cry little girl, sigh little one
He's not the last in the world let your guard back up...
Because love never lasts...

   - Toni

My sister's keeper

She craves attention
As though it's her last meal
She begs for someone to see her
And when they meet her, they mistreat her
I tried to warn her, but it's like she doesn't get it
Told her about the world and all the wolves that are in it
She becomes their prey, they become her love
Naïve to believe that she is the only one
She holds on to his words, to his lies she is blinded
And when the bastard hurts her
Guess who's left to fix it?

- Toni

Yesterday when you cried

Yesterday
I watched you cry
I wiped the tears
From your eyes
I wonder why
You let him do this to you
Should I take this baby
He doesn't need to see
The things you do
Quit lying
Your life isn't ready for this
How could I
Just see the pain in his eyes
And walk away
With a lonely goodbye

- De'Vray

Epiphany to grow

If I had an epiphany
Would I see
That it was you
Who deceived me?
Telling me Yarved
"Take it easy, it'll be okay, just wait till another day"
But was it not
Supposed to be resolved yesterday?
What's the reason
You're trying to procrastinate
Combine my feelings
With my motivation
Clouded my vision
Because I sat there in anticipation
For the best
But what I got was far worse
Than I expected

- De'Vray

A time in history

There was a time
I wasn't proud
To be who I am
There wasn't a place
Where I felt safe
To be who I am
There was a school
That I was talked about in
Just for the thought
Of being who I am
But looking back
Now is the time
Here is the place
Where I break
Out of my shell and be proud
Because yes I am
A bi-sexual, African-American male
But I am also human
So why should I feel
Like an abomination
Because of a book
That contradicts itself?
Don't get me wrong

Yes, I am a Christian
And a God-fearing man
But does that mean if He knew me
Before I was even born
That I shouldn't be
Who He has already
Paved my destiny to be
But there go those
Overly Christian saints
Jumping at my throat
Committing their own sin
Just to solve this one
And just like that holy book reads
"No sin is greater
 Than another"

- De'Vray

Reasons for my actions

You see my body
Cause you destroyed
My self esteem
You see the way I dressed
Everything matches
From underwear to shoelace
You see that I'm single
Because I'm afraid
For you to judge me
About who I choose to be with
God can only judge me
But that's at the end
We are just beginning
How can I find myself?
When I'm trying to be someone else
You put me in this
Contradictory lifestyle
And I can't escape
Because no matter
How hard I try
It's starting to define me

- De'Vray

I spoke

I spoke of pain
You assumed I meant
From the game
I spoke of love
And you assumed
That I'm too young
But if I smile and laugh
You tell me "that a boy"
Like these fake emotions
Can hide these scars
That even time
Couldn't heal

- De'Vray

My Blessings

When you floated down from heaven
My world would forever be bright
Sadness has subsided, and LOVE has slayed hate
My heart is permanently in your possession
My soul was destined to match with yours
Missing for all these years
The piece to this puzzle is now connected
At last, the dream I've prayed to be real
The wish on the star I've hoped to come true
Has become reality in my eyes
And if you ever left me
Half of me would no longer be alive

- Toni

Remember her?

Behind her eyes, she begs to be seen
To be heard for once!
That's all she wants
Yet, everyone
Turns a deaf ear to her constant pleas
Can't you see inside of her?
The way her soul bleeds?
All she needs is understanding
A little bit of compassion
She doesn't need your sympathy
This girl needs empathy
She contemplates, seizing away
A life she never got to see
If you've forgotten who she was
That girl... she is me....

- Toni

If I could only pretend

My only mission in life
Is to make my parents proud
And become the best woman I can be
This proves problematic
Because I'm more consumed in my own insecurities
I have not the slightest idea of who I am
Believing in me seems difficult
Because I am a stranger to myself
So how can I count on the world to see me as perfect
When my flaws are evident especially to me?
Every question I ask myself
Lingers in my mind unanswered
At this time, this point in life
Becoming someone else works out successfully
At least, for the popular people
I mean, they receive whatever they desire
Just by pretending to be confident
So, maybe I'll give that poker face a try

- Toni

I wonder why

I could feel the coldness of his heart
As he held me against him
So, I wonder why I didn't take that as a sign
I didn't see a light in his eyes as he looked upon me
So, I wonder why I didn't take that as a sign
I waited till he took from me
The very precious gift God has given me
Before I realized he was a demon in disguise
He used my body as a television
Once he'd gotten tired
He turned me off and fell asleep

~ Toni

Perplexing

Sometimes, I feel as though my mouth is betraying me
The words that come out, are failing to convey
The thoughts I surely intend to say
And the sentiment deep within me is
Hiding behind this gate
This gate I call a guard
Because I don't know any other way
To express my temperament
I want to say I'm sorry
For being unable to tell you
What's been in my head all along
It just gets tiresome to regularly say
"I'm fine, I'm okay"

~ Toni

Armed

With my pen and paper
Yes I'm armed and ready
When is enough, enough?
If I take a gun
And aim it at everyone
So now you pretend
To care about my pain
But your words are vain
Because where was that care
In my elementary years
When I was
Called gay
Forced to hear them
Mock my name
Those days...
That made me
Into the sociopath
That I am today
I just want to say
Thank you for being there
When I needed your protection

- De'Vray

Feel?

How would you feel if someone looked at you
With that much hate
How would you feel if someone looked at you
As if you're a disgrace
Tell me how you would feel
If you had this pain
Put on your shoulders
How would you feel
If you had the weight
Of the world
The weight of all
Your past mistakes
Crashing down on your soul
How would you feel
If you had the burden
Of feeling you've done
So much wrong that no matter
If you repent
Or even sugar coat the call
In His sons holy name
That God still sends you to voicemail

- De'Vray

Pay me no mind

They pay attention
To what they want to see
They listen
Only to the things
They want to hear
And when it comes down to it
The truth is never clear
Was it fear?
That brought about this curse
Lack of confidence
Makes me feel
Like I'm better off
Returning to the dirt

- De'Vray

Forget the pain

Going to numb myself
Because the pain I felt
Just may overwhelm me
Who can I turn to?
When everybody's looking to me
To guide them
Forget the pain
How could we?
The pain helped to shape
Our individuality

- De'Vray

Explaining him

Yarved isn't dead
He lives within me
Ain't it crazy
Two souls in one body
Was this part of Gods plan
Or am I just a man
That fell into the Devils hands

- De'Vray

My nemesis: Death

One day, I will have to face my enemy
His name is Death
And he has already met many others
I'm praying
It'll be a while before he greets my mother
I'd rather face him myself, toe to toe
Then allow him to take her by the hand
Ask him to come again sometime later
Tell him that I would fight him if I get the chance
If he stares me in the face
I'd tell him to stay away!
Beg him to harass someone else's life
I just need a little more time!
On my knees to God
I ask, if he could fend Death off a little while longer
So I could prove to the ones I love
That I can be better, I will do better
Until they're lives are, and will become
What they always dreamed of

- Toni

This is who I am

I know lately, the things that I've been saying
Has got you all confused
I mean, my mood swings are pretty frequent these days
You're probably thinking that I'm insane
Hear me out, I promise
I'll figure this out
I'll gather all my notions, my ideas and my beliefs
I'll put on a smile and tell you how much I love you
And that I'm perfectly normal
Kiss your lips and go about my day
In a few weeks or so
I'll have another episode
But, you've been warned, so now you know

- Toni

The silent Killer: Depression

I'm usually unprepared when it afflicts me
The misty heat runs unexpectedly
It's a voiceless miserable routine
Where tears form in my eyes for no obvious reason
Converting into sobs and heaving
Heavy breathing
Collapsing to the floor
It dominates me
I am left speculating what this could be
Looking into the mirror
I discover the silent killer, was within me

- Toni

Revolution

The wave lengths of my brain
Reasons that, if I start this WAR
The amount of bodies on the BATTLEFIELD
Will reproduce an army of WARRIORS

In translation:
My mind is warning me
That if I break his heart
The amount of pain I will cause
May create a man with a cold exterior

    -   Toni

The human experience

The human brain
Is a workplace for thoughts to take place
If every idea cooperates with the other
This may generate an assembly of inspirations
We all inspire to be the Ambassador of our own beliefs
Having a voice in society means
Being an individual in a world of conformants
Most folks rather fit in with the bunch as "we"
Rather than classify themselves "I"
In my opinion, I am the R.E.B.E.L of this domain

~ Toni

Realization

It feels like
You just hit my heart
With a truck
Now I'm stuck with this feeling
It's not love or hate
But I never thought
That in hours, minutes, seconds
This life that you see
As so precious
Could be taken away
Like it never existed

- De'Vray

I wish words were undefinable

Words have never
Been just words
And when they define you
No matter how strong you are
You feel a certain burden
Has been placed on you
This I couldn't help but show
When I hung my head low
And I confide within myself
Because in that moment
In those words
You had taken away my hope
Made me feel as if I was alone
Even though I laughed at your jokes
To hide myself behind closed doors
It makes me wonder
Am I in need of therapy
Because I'm crazy?
Or because I need to build self-esteem
But if I am crazy
I wonder is society to blame
Because I wasn't born this way

- De'Vray

Observing the pain

I stepped back
And glanced
Look at how he plays with her emotions
He comes, then he leaves
A constant heart break
This leaves
Her and me
She went to sleep
On a cloud hoping
To wake up in his arms
I can only pray that she
Continues to keep dreaming,
Because reality is Heaven's nightmare

- De'Vray

Heaven is smiling down

You made me feel secure
I know you wanted
The best for me
I wish I could have told you before
That you're my hero
You loved me
When no one else
But God could
You cared for me
When no one else would
You're the reason
Why I smile uncontrollably
When I look up at the sky
I know you're looking back at me
Because sometimes
It's like I can hear you
Saying that you're proud of me
And the man that you
Helped mold
For me to be

- De'Vray

Staying put

Dreams of the top
No fear of the bottom
Only nightmares
Of staying in the middle
That's a tragedy
I cannot face
One that I hope
I shall never
Have to embrace
Because staying still
With the option of up or down
Would have my mind racing
A powerful choice
That could change my life
For better or for worse

- De'Vray

Absolution

I used drugs as an excuse
To ease the pain
I used hate in substitute
Of saying "I'm vulnerable"
There was no other way
To hide the shame
As I felt each dagger
That spat from my mouth
And punctured your heart
Forgive me, is what I wanted to say

- Toni

If you can hear me, come back

"Don't do this"
I beg you
You looked at me as though you misheard me
"Think it over"
I pleaded
You turned away and paced the floor
"Look at me"
I commanded
And in your eyes
The person I once knew
Disappeared
"Where are you?"
I asked
You say nothing
Holding your face in my hands
A tear crept its way in your eye
In relief
I hold you close
Hoping you'll come back to me

- Toni

The ocean of eternity

She has tried everything
Said almost anything
To keep him from the ledge
She couldn't and wouldn't
Allow him to be so selfish
How could he leave her
In this world
When there's no one else like him?
She couldn't fathom his reasons
For wanting to end it all
She gave him more love
Than his parents could ever give him
She provided the necessities
He needed to survive
Affection, care, understanding
And most importantly love
Confusion, is what she felt
When she watched him walk towards the edge
She tried hard to stop him
But he resisted each attempt
He stepped one foot in front
And she ran to grab his hand
Gazing into each other's souls
He felt the impact of hers

As one, they jumped off the ledge
   Into the ocean of eternity

   - Toni

If God reads minds

If God reads minds
He'd probably be disappointed
Perhaps 40% of my day
Begins with an appreciation of His grace
And a "Thank you God"
And the other 60% consists of
Sinful preoccupations
I will not justify my behavior
And I'm more than certain
That my dirty deeds
Will haunt me as I mature
Childish things such as: cursing, drinking and
Other reckless conduct
Will no longer be as important to me
I live for today and anticipate tomorrow
But, for now, in my youth
Fun to me will always be reckless
So, if God reads minds
At least He'll know, I'm working on
Myself everyday

   - Toni

FPD (Friendship Police Department)

Betrayal is the crime you have committed
Anger is the emotion I feel
Tension is the aura surrounding us
The atmosphere is thick
My mood is devious
Grasping the whole concept of you
Stepping a foot upon my back
As I went down from despair
Has got my heart pounding in my chest
At a DUI speeding rate
I wish there was an FPD (friendship police department)
To arrest you for your unspeakable crime
Animosity is the reaction
It's continuing to defile my face in distaste

- Toni

Friends disappear

You put it on everything you loved
That you would be there
Where are you?
You pinky promised
Crossed your heart
And hoped to die
That our love, our friendship
That it would last forever
I pray to God
That you're not six feet under
But was I a fool
Did you delude me
Into believing that you
Actually cared for me
It's just so strange
How things change
In just a few short
    Days

- De'Vray

Love is what they said

They told me
To learn how to love
I told them to love me
And the feeling would be returned
But I'm still here
Lost with no emotion
I thought you said you cared
Maybe I should be more careful
Of whom I trust
With my expectations
Too high there was no where
Else to go but down
So I'm surprised
That I'm surprised you failed me

- De'Vray

Stand

I stand alone in fear
Of being me
23+23 made one
But I feel
Like it's just me created
To be left
Who can I turn to?
When the people
I look up to
Keep turning their back
On me

- De'Vray

Worry in my soul

This pain within me
That haunts me
Not only in my nightmares
But in my dreams
It makes me worry
About myself
More than anyone could ever see
No one but me
Could see these demons
That have made a home
Within me
Witness them tie down my soul
And take away my hope
If I close my eyes
I realize that not only the church
But society
Has been blind to me

- De'Vray

Different life

My life's its own apocalypse
Can't no one stop this sin
That's growing inside of me
God will You forgive me
After all the wrong I did
Should I serve
A life sentence in purgatory
Thoughts I can't hide from
Dreams I can't run from
Screams I can't pretend
That I don't know where
Their coming from
People can't see where
I'm coming from
Now I'm knocking on satan's door
Cause his house is now my home

- De'Vray

Captivated

Woe me no longer
Every care in the world is invested into one factor
Him
But, almost for a second
We could've lost it as soon as we found it
Discovering love in a place where youth meets lust
Him and I
Became inseparable with our eyes
It seems we wanted that word called love
For the wrong reasons
Until we met each other's personalities
And when the two clashed
We shattered each other's heart
Breaking up with one another
Just because
Now, there's no coincidence
Because we lasted through the aches
We've found each other in love
Instead of lust
For the first time

- Toni

My conscious

Little girl
Quit sitting in that closet!
Hiding from your problems
As though they've been chasing you your whole life
Little girl don't let those tears go to waste
Wipe them away with your hand
And suck it up
There are people out there waiting to judge you
You need to put a smile on your face
Pretend to be content
At least you'll be making an effort
Instead of running to that dark place
In the closet where the bad memories haunt you
Oh yes they'll be inside you forever
Have no hope for your future being in peace
Little girl
Lose those thoughts of a life with no hostility
Rid yourself of the thoughts of having
A life of zero pain
The world is gonna crush once you step
Foot on your own
Where's your friends?
You don't have one in the world
Because you allow me to rule your mind

Little girl
Uncoil yourself from that shell and lie with your smile
I know it hurts but, keep your eyes dry for
The rest of your life

- Toni

To the burdened man

I never seen so much shame
In one man's face
As I seen it in yours
But I want you to know
That no matter how many mistakes you've made
And the anguish of knowing no matter
How hard you've tried
You still feel as though you've accomplished nothing
I want you to know that it's not your fault
You've just gotten stuck with an unwanted fate
That there's a time for you to prove
That you've done all you could
To show your family you loved them and that
You've tried everything
But, the most important thing
Is that you're still working on yourself
To be an image of God

- Toni

To the burdened woman

I want to praise you
For working so hard to become an
Example for your children
Though, you're not in a place that you chose
This life chose you
Because God mostly gives the struggling
Women the true faith
You could've lost your way, but fought through it all
The sleepless nights, the hardships and strife
You ran through the rain to face the storm
And you made it out alive
You deserve a crown, for filling a man's shoes
For being a mother who would do all that's
Necessary for survival
By all means you're a queen,
You're strong beyond measure
The true inspiration comes from a person who's
Been through and seen the toughest times
Who has survived and still holds faith
In one God

- Toni

Right through you

I see a scared child, behind your lifeless eyes
Inside your icy heart, I see a warm side
Sheltered in your soul, dim by sight
I see a helpless child, doused in light

- Toni

Closed emotions

You look at me
Like I'm the one to blame
If you hadn't kept
Your mouth shut
We wouldn't be forced
To guess your thoughts
When it comes to your
Feelings and emotions
You care
Not to share
So how dare
You blame us
As if this is just
What we put you through
You left us with nothing
To believe in
So shame on us because we decided
Not to follow in your footsteps
Leave the child we helped birth
But the lights are off
Oh what we would uncover
If we came out of the dark
    - De'Vray

I see me

I look into his eyes
And they're full of lies
I can only wonder why
Why you want to make
The same mistake
I look into his tears
Pain and fear
Drenched his face
I worry that he will face
This struggle through his adolescence
I listened to him scream
I can still hear it in my dreams
I looked in the mirror
And saw him starring
Back at me

- De'Vray

All I know

How can I let go when all I know
How to do
Is hold on
Hold on for my life's sake
Hold on to make it through
The day's mistakes
Am I trapped in fear?
Of letting go?
What would happen?
If I took that leap
And didn't bother to hold on to anything
I wonder would It?
Could it?
Corrupt me even more

- De'Vray

She makes me feel

My baby
Makes me feel
Like I'm slim shady
Telling everybody
I think my dad's gone crazy
No baby I'm not crazy
I'm just standing on the other side
Of societies understanding

   - De'Vray

Maybe I am

I am not blind
To any of my actions
Maybe I am
The main stressor
Of my fading mental capacity
It's not something
I do on purpose
Lack of will
Has left me unfocused

- De'Vray

Money can't buy dreams

Dreams money can't buy
Should I believe?
That money can
Buy anything
Especially in the economy
In which we live?
Should I believe that?
If I work for a big corporation
That my pay checks
Will buy me true happiness
But these dreams
That I have
It's funny because these dreams
Are dreams money can't buy

- De'Vray

I begged for your hand

With the weight of the world upon me
You watched as I fell to your feet
With all the strength left in me
I lifted my head,
 and with my eyes
I begged for your hand
Shedding a tear,
hoping for assistance
I crawled onto my knees
And begged again
You watched me intently
I waited pitifully
Then, with my last bit of dignity
I stood upon my trembling knees
Staring into your face
I held my pride upon my back
Realizing that
Only I can
Pull myself to my feet again

    - Toni

I shouldn't care

I care
Which is making me
Emotionally
And mentally
Unstable
But how can I be stable
Help me stop these tears
And just tell me why
Because all this drama
Has left me in pain
And it hurts to breathe
I hate feeling like I need
The feeling of those
Dead trees
To make me happy
And to make me love myself

- De'Vray

Fading sun

I've had worse days
But it's like the sun
Just faded from my life
And when I look into her eyes
All I see is empty promises
And broken dreams
As I watch those tears
Stream down her face
Like a fiery rain
God I wish I could help
But only she controls
Her fate

- De'Vray

Words are true?

If your words were true
As you say mine aren't
Why has "I love you?"
Strayed so far away
And left you speechless
At the sight of the man
I am today
Yet if you loved me
You would know what to say
If you loved me
You wouldn't treat me this way

- De'Vray

Mistakes made

Still I rise on my own
Here I stand all alone
Even though I'd rather
Be in my bed
In my own home
But my don't give a care actions
Made me believe
Who needs life?
And now death
Is right around the corner
And I'm staring into this gun
Begging God to let me see
My daughter
One last time
Because out of everything
I was a good father

- De'Vray

Contradiction amendment

Am I seen as crazy?
Because in societies eyes
I shouldn't stand up
For what I believe
But is it not society
That saw fit
That under the first amendment
For me to be obligated to freedom of speech
And as a poet
Should I not
Use that to the
Fullest extent
Of the law?
Am I wrong?

- De'Vray

I remember

You were there
Laughing at me
My pain
My emotions
Back when words
Were just letters
Put together
Back when writing
Was just something fun
That I was good at
But now these words
These letters
Are the only thing
That frees my soul
From those stones
That my childhood pain
Buried me under

- De'Vray

I wish you would

I wish that
You would talk to me
And tell me where I stand
Am I alone?
And on my own
Or are you still there?
My silence
Lead to violence
That I understand
But my love for you
Lead to my heart racing
My mind spinning
Sick all the time
And contemplating
SUICIDE

- De'Vray

Who are you?

What if my gender
Had been female
Then the way I am
Would be accepted right
Cause then
Its girl on girl
Not male on male
And in these hormonal
High schoolers eyes
That would make me sexier
But in societies eye
We're free
To be in their captivity
Because the bible says
We're an abomination
But who are you to say
That I'm not bisexual, gay by nature

- De'Vray

My heart beat

˄
‾ ‾‾‾‾‾

This is my heart beat
When I'm near you
It's not because I'm nervous
Or afraid
It's because you make me feel deceased
You stop my heart cold
With your icy spiteful words
You kill my soul a little bit at a time
My hope is long gone
Love has strayed too far away
Life always comes to an end
You always have something to say!
But today I am speaking up with these
Few words: "I have nothing to say to you"
As your face races with shock
My body moves I don't have to talk
You know what happened after that
I left you there
˄ ˄ ˄ ˄
‾ ‾ ‾ ‾
My heart beats easier now
Because I am no longer terrified to say "NO"!

- De'Vray

A joke pushed too far

Hey De'Vray
Can you hear me?
Your eyes are closed
And I can't feel a pulse
Come on bro
Wake up the jokes over
I didn't know
The smile on your face
Was to cover up the heartache
Come on De'Vray
Wake up
The game is over
I know you want to go
But Daddy's not calling
You home just yet
Dear God,
Help my brother
To these people
He was one they
Could never understand
Lord I know you hear me
This is your son Yarved
I promise if you wake him up
I'll try my best

To never let him
Be hurt again
-Amen-

- De'Vray

Holding interest

Was I blinded?
By my insecurities
It's funny how
I still hold interest in you
Even after all the drama
That you put me through
Even though all I want
To do is make you
Smile and you,
You treat me like
I'm trash
Sitting on the corner
I swear if I can
I'll never let you treat me
Like this again

- De'Vray

Don't care assumptions

So I don't care
It's funny how
Your assumptions
Are so far out there
It's funny how
Your presumption of me
Is one that is not fair
It's dumb how I can't sleep
Because you're not here
It's crazy
That I'm fifteen and I still can't bare
To see you weak
To see you weep
To see you sick
Oh God
I swear
To see you in a hospital bed
Is something I fear

- De'Vray

Attacking my emotions

Consider this an attack
On my self-conscious
You felt the guilt
From the lack of protection
Now you feel hurt
Because your pride has to be swallowed
To save your only children
This is mindless behavior
My sight, all along I knew it was right
But the same guilt
You felt on your shoulders
Solemnly rest on my heart
I want your attention
I wanted more of your love
We wanted more than protection
We need more than you could fathom
You look back and only see
The hurt in our eyes
The anger scorched in our souls
And the spite that makes our words
Seem wise today
What we feel
Only seemed important

When it related to the past event
That changed our childish mentality
But honestly trying to change our past
Might have messed up our future
As a whole, as a family
We are lost because now
We are divided but the love I have
For you and her makes me keep trying
To keep us united
As you feel that this is a war
That you're fighting on your own for us
Consider the fact
That we're fighting wars
With the demons in us
Fighting wars, with the pain
That refuses to leave us
War on our lives
Because it felt like not only you
But heaven has neglected us
Without thought of the reaction
That would scar our lives forever
This misconception has left me
On the battlefield with no weapon

- De'Vray

My mommy

One day
He can say
My mommy's been through a lot
She went through hell with men
And came out still trying to love again
She went through
Both types of abuse
And still refused
To bow down to these egotistical fools

One day
As he stands in class
He can say
My mommy went through a lot
So that I could be here today

- De'Vray

How . . .

How do you lose trust
When there was none
To begin with
No one wants to claim
The wrong
That they all had a hand in
Because in everybody's eyes
They're right
And to accept they're wrong
Would just lead to neglect
Which leaves us back at square one
Making an exception

- De'Vray

Saying errors

Words are cheap
It's the context
In which you use them
That pays the bills
Writing is a passion
That is getting old
Because there are boundaries
In which I want to go
But society
Has forbid me to even hint of
Like if I speak on politics
I better be politically correct
If I spoke on abortion
Then I would need more than just facts
To back up my opinion
But honestly in my opinion
Society is corrupt
That's why words are cheap
And this writing is only a passion
Because if I speak on these issues
There would be nothing
To pay the bills
   - De'Vray

Yarved speaks

When I came into this world
My only name was
De'Vray C. Rogers
But I have lost him and now I speak
With this aching pain in me
For me to survive
I need him to come back
But these voices tell me
Yarved your life is easy
But these people are blind
Meaning they cannot see
What happens when those doors
Close behind me
They don't see that smile, fade from my face
They don't see the razor in my hand
Or the pain that made that same hand
    SHAKE
God I'm sorry but they bound my soul
With chains that were so tight
That now that you have released me
I still feel them when I In-hale
And it hurts
  - De'Vray

I am isolated

Isolated
So late
To the fact
That I cannot AWAKE
Or come into the light
Of my own past mistakes

- De'Vray

Crush

I'm crushed
So you can't be sad
When all my dreams
Crumbled
I'm broken
So you can't get mad
When my heart
Shattered

- De'Vray

Never would I

Even though
I have feminine ways
I am nothing short of a man
Even if it's true that I'm gay
There is no way
I would let you treat me this way
Although I do have class
I would still politely
Knock you on your ass
It will be a rainy day in hell
Before I let you treat me this way
People like you are the reason
Yarved came into play

- De'Vray

Giving up

I'm heartless and cold
I used to want a reason
To hold on
But now I've got all the reason to let go
You've never had your parents
Throw you out
Like you didn't matter
You've never had your parents
turn their backs on you
when it really mattered

- De'Vray

You want

You want to be at the top
But you left your priorities
At the bottom
So focused on things
That didn't matter
That you forgot
About the things that did

- De'Vray

How do you heal?

You can't try to heal
When you don't know what to do
You can't try to love
When you never learned how to
How could I forgive?
When you're giving me
Every reason not to
Why should I let go?
When you're giving me
 every reason to hold on
 How can I trust you?
When trust was broken
at the first touch
at the first tear
the first time you condoned
wrongful actions
yes I know it hurts
but your children's scream
you can't seem to hear anymore
even though we could never cope
tears are something
we now fear to let flow
you can see others pain
but you can't seem to see

or maybe you don't want to see
the depth of ours
hell could be home
cause pain is something
that is well known
in this household

- De'Vray

Mother

When I think of you
My body shakes
Although we fuss and fight
No matter what
your love
Is the only thing
That keeps me from falling apart

    Sincerely,
       De'Vray

Scars

I got scars even time couldn't heal
 Only I could reveal
 But if I told my soul, they would kill

De'Vray

Not alone

Victim
I'm not the only one
Just the only one to speak up
When did breaking rules
Become cool again
I fell victim
To the fame, power
I fell victim
To the ego they built up
Till it was too much to handle
And then they pushed it on my shoulders
Built me for destruction
But my only purpose
Was to serve these words
I pray they're served correctly

- De'Vray

Once

I was once a boy
That taught himself
how to be a man
forget a father figure
ever since the world
slapped me with reality
cause in reality
I may stumble
But I refuse to fall
Just cause I give up
Doesn't mean I still don't stand tall
I am not just a writer

- De'Vray

Life as a misfit

So I'm sadistic
Because all my life
I've been a misfit
Open your eyes
You'll see this new kid
On the block
Talked about because of his skin
And because he prefers
Women and men
Can you tell me?
What is this kid to do
When the school system
Has marked him as unruly
His own family
Believes that this
Enraged, short tempered beast
Is who he wants to be?
Yet even though
He has destroyed all hope for his life
No one tried to help
No one gave a damn about his feelings
So now why should
He gives a damn about his health
Why should he care?

About one day achieving great wealth
And you can only wonder
What goes on in his head
Wonder why
His life is so full of corruption

- De'Vray

Strength in words
Pain in meanings Pt. II

Who put your hands around my throat
Who forced you to throw me out
In the blistering cold
What made you right for blaming me
For supposedly tying your hands
How did I give you no other option
Because before I can remember
You've been laying your hands on me
You have physically & emotionally abused me
How can you still look me in my eyes
And tell me that you love me
I forgave you the first time
Only because you didn't know
But your action were repeated
So I began to lose hope
Now that I don't trust you
You want to complain about it
But did I complain about the emotional scars
That you alone put on my soul
Tell me why I should trust you
Just because you're my mother?
No, that won't stand as a reason
Because you were also supposed to be

My hero, my protector, my care giver
But you were on the other side of the battlefield
Taking shots at me
You claim you're fighting for me
But I'm only breathing
Because of who?
I hope you can finally see
Why I have so many trust issues
And why I have a hard time
Trusting you

www.ingramcontent.com/pod-product-compliance
Lightning Source LLC
Chambersburg PA
CBHW031353040426
42444CB00005B/279